HOMES

By Joanna Brundle

KidHaven
PUBLISHING

A Look at Life Around the World

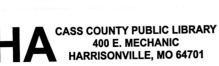

Published in 2019 by
KidHaven Publishing, an Imprint of Greenhaven Publishing, LLC
353 3rd Avenue
Suite 255
New York, NY 10010

Designer: Jasmine Pointer
Editor: Kirsty Holmes

Photocredits: Abbreviations: l-left, r-right, b-bottom, t-top, c-center, m-middle. All images are courtesy of Shutterstock.com. With thanks to Getty Images, Thinkstock Photo and iStockphoto. Front cover – Salvador Aznar, Sam DCruz, Ewelina Wachala. 2 – eFesenko. 4l – Attila JANDI. 4r – Firdouss Ross Rosli. 5t – Monkey Business Images. 5b – StockPhotosArt. 6 – Luciano Mortula - LGM. 7 – f11photo. 8l – Angelinalee. 8r – EcoPrint. 9 – meunierd. 10 – Laura Martinelli. 11 – Sergejs Filimon. 12t – Bondarenco Vladimir. 12b – esbobeldijk. 13t – Olga Kashubin. 13b – my nordic. 14t – Nicolas Ulmer. 14b – Belovodchenko Anton. 15 – Balate Dorin. 16 – Alicia G. Monedero. 17t – Lucy Brown - loca4motion. 17b – Katiekk. 18t – ashadhodhomei. 18b – Ijam Hairi. 19 – pikselstock. 20tr – Kjersti Joergensen. 20b – Byelikova Oksana. 21t – Click Images. 21b – Dr. J. Beller. 22l – Wong Hock weng. 22r – Tony Campbell.

All facts, statistics, web addresses and URLs in this book were verified as valid and accurate at time of writing. No responsibility for any changes to external websites or references can be accepted by either the author or publisher.

Cataloging-in-Publication Data

Names: Brundle, Joanna.
Title: Homes / Joanna Brundle.
Description: New York : KidHaven Publishing, 2019. | Series: A look at life around the world | Includes glossary and index.
Identifiers: ISBN 9781534528512 (pbk.) | ISBN 9781534528536 (library bound) | ISBN 9781534528529 (6 pack) | ISBN 9781534528543 (ebook)
Subjects: LCSH: Dwellings--Juvenile literature.
Classification: LCC GT172.B78 2019 | DDC 392.3'6--dc23

Printed in the United States of America

CPSIA compliance information: Batch #BW19KL: For further information contact Greenhaven Publishing LLC, New York, New York at 1-844-317-7404.

Please visit our website, www.greenhavenpublishing.com. For a free color catalog of all our high-quality books, call toll free 1-844-317-7404 or fax 1-844-317-7405.

CONTENTS

Words that look like this can be found in the glossary on page 23.

ALL KINDS OF HOMES

People live in all kinds of homes. In this book, we will be traveling around the world, looking at the homes of children just like you. As you read, think about how the homes we visit are similar to your home and how they are different.

These strange houses, called the Cube Houses, are in Rotterdam, Netherlands.

This traditional longhouse in Borneo is home to lots of families who all live together.

4

Home is a place to eat, sleep, play, and be with the people you love.

Casa de Penedo
(House of Stone), Portugal

This unusual home is built between four huge boulders.

People make their homes in all sorts of places, using many different <u>materials</u>. Homes can be on land, on water, or even on wheels. Some people live high in the mountains. Others live in caves under the ground. Wherever you live, home should be a place where you feel comfortable and safe.

CITY HOMES

In cities, there might not be much space to build homes. Tall buildings have layers of apartments, built one on top of the other. This means they take up less space on the ground. Apartment buildings often have no yards. Some have a shared yard that is used by all the residents.

Around 38 million people live in Tokyo. It is one of the most crowded cities in the world.

Shantytowns in Brazil are called favelas. They are found on the edges of Brazil's cities.

Favela, Rio de Janeiro, Brazil

Many people who live in cities around the world are very poor and live in areas called shantytowns. They build small shacks from things they find on the streets or at garbage dumps. The shacks have no electricity, toilets, or running water.

HOMES IN THE COUNTRYSIDE

Dorze huts have to be built very tall – <u>termites</u> eat away the base, so they gradually get shorter and shorter!

This home in Namibia is made of wood with a thatched roof of dried grasses.

Homes in the countryside are often built from natural materials, including local stone, timber, and grasses. The Dorze people of Chencha, Ethiopia, build their tall huts from the bamboo and banana plants that grow nearby. Dorze huts look sort of like an elephant, with a "trunk" forming the entrance.

The Zulu people of South Africa build dome-shaped homes called iQukwane. The men collect the sticks and the women bind them together using plaited reeds and grasses. A tree trunk in the center helps it stay up.

Countryside homes often have land around them that is used as <u>grazing</u> for animals or for growing crops.

CAVE HOMES

Goreme is a town in Turkey where people live in caves. The caves have been carved into rocks that were formed when <u>volcanoes</u> erupted three million years ago. People have lived in these cave homes for hundreds of years. Some of the homes have been turned into restaurants and hotels for <u>tourists</u>.

The cave homes now have running water and electricity.

Cave homes are warm in winter and cool in the hot Spanish summers.

Almost half the people in the town of Guadix in southern Spain live underground in cave homes. The caves were dug out of the rock by hand hundreds of years ago. Some of the cave homes are over a thousand years old.

ECO HOMES

Eco Home, Sweden

Eco homes are made to be friendly to the environment. This means that they use less of the world's precious <u>resources</u>, such as water and electricity.

Huge windows make good use of the sun's light and heat.

Solar panels fitted to the roof of a house take in sunlight. They change it into electricity that can be used in the home.

Wind Turbines

Solar Panels

City apartment buildings are sometimes planted with green walls, also known as living walls. Plants grow in all directions to cover the outside walls. Green wall gardens provide <u>habitats</u> for birds and insects. They also help to <u>insulate</u> the apartments so that they use less electricity.

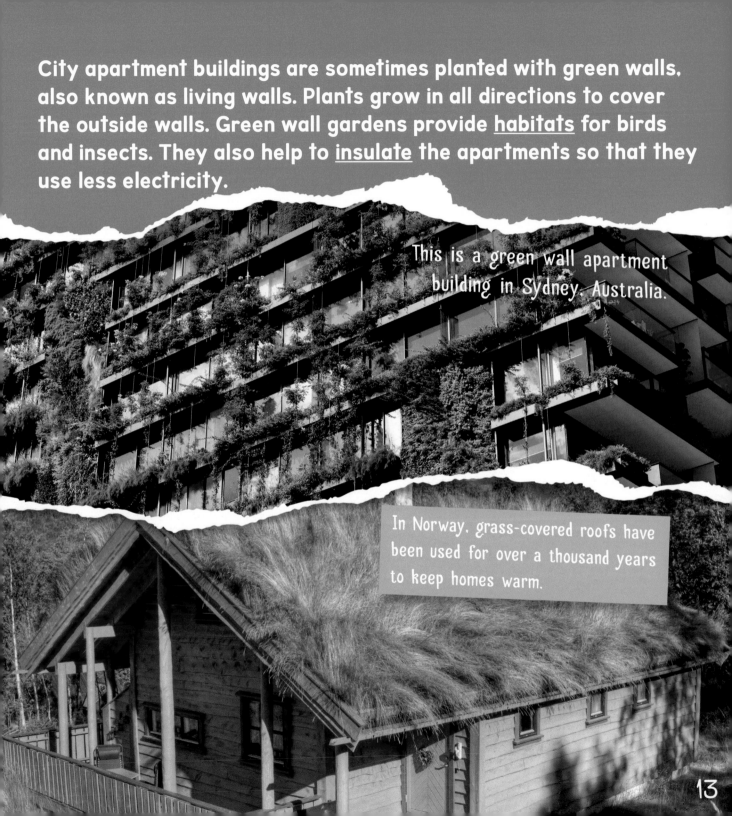

This is a green wall apartment building in Sydney, Australia.

In Norway, grass-covered roofs have been used for over a thousand years to keep homes warm.

HOMES IN COLD AND HOT PLACES

Homes in snowy places often have sloping roofs that overhang the building. Snow is very heavy and this shape of roof helps the snow slide off easily.

Mountain Home in the French Alps

The Inuit people of Greenland and Canada build igloos as temporary homes in the winter or as shelters when they are out hunting.

Igloos are dome-shaped and built with blocks of snow. "Igloo" is the Inuit word for home.

Homes in hot countries are often painted white. This helps to keep them cool, because white reflects the heat of the sun. They are often built of stone or a material called <u>adobe</u>. Adobe dries hard and keeps the homes cool inside.

Whitewashed Homes in Mykonos, Greece

HOMES ON THE MOVE

Canal boats were once used to move goods such as coal and wood around the United Kingdom. The boats are called narrowboats because they were built to fit along the narrow canals in the area. Today, many people make their home on these boats, traveling from place to place.

Narrowboats now have an engine, but were originally pulled by a horse on the riverbank.

The door of a ger is always painted blue or orange and decorated with patterns.

The <u>nomads</u> of Mongolia live in round tents called gers. Gers have a wooden frame with a felt cover. Animal skins and ropes made of horse tail hair hold everything together. Gers can be easily taken down and set up when the families move on to find fresh grazing for their animals.

HOMES NEAR WATER

The Bajau people of Malaysia spend all their time living and working on the ocean. Some live in handmade houseboats, called lepa-lepa. Others live in huts on stilts, built over the sea. They use small boats to visit other huts or to come to the shore.

A Bajau Houseboat

A Bajau Hut on Stilts

This is a floating island and home on Lake Titicaca.

The Uros people have been living on the lake for hundreds of years.

The Uros people of Peru and Bolivia live on floating islands on Lake Titicaca. The islands and their homes are made from the reeds that grow around the edges of the lake. As the reeds rot at the bottom of the islands, new reeds must be added to the top.

UNUSUAL HOMES

Burj Khalifa in Dubai is one of the tallest buildings in the world. It is 2,717 feet (828 m) tall and home to about 1,800 people who live in its 900 apartments.

Most of the homes in the city of Jodhpur, India, are painted blue. Nobody knows for sure why this is so!

Blue may have been chosen because it is the color of the god Shiva, whose followers have lived in Jodhpur throughout history.

This house in Wales is the smallest house in Great Britain at 6 feet (1.8 m) wide.

These homes are built on a steep overhanging cliff in Corsica, France.

ANIMAL HOMES

The place where an animal lives is called its habitat. Just like us, animals need a safe place to sleep and raise their young.

Weaver Birds, Africa

Weaver birds build their nests from grasses and leaves.

African Penguins, Boulders Beach, South Africa

These penguins build a nest by scooping out a hollow in the sand.

GLOSSARY

adobe	a type of clay
grazing	land where animals feed on grass
habitats	the natural homes of animals or plants
insulate	cover something with a material that stops heat loss
materials	substances used to make something
nomads	people who do not live in one place
resources	things that are of use or value
shantytowns	areas on the edges of cities where people live in shacks they have made themselves
termites	insects that live together in a large group in a mound of earth
tourists	people who visit a place for pleasure
volcanoes	openings in the Earth's surface that can erupt ash, gas, and very hot liquid rock

INDEX